First U.S. edition 2007

Library of Congress Cataloging-in-Publication Data is available.
Library of Congress Catalog Card Number pending
ISBN 978-0-7636-3558-9

10 9 8 7 6 5 4 3 2 1

Printed in China

This book was typeset in ITCKabel.
The illustrations were created digitally.

Candlewick Press
2067 Massachusetts Avenue
Cambridge, Massachusetts 02140

visit us at www.candlewick.com

CANDLEWICK PRESS
CAMBRIDGE, MASSACHUSETTS

For Poppy and Finn

The author and publisher would like to thank Sue Ellis at
the Centre for Literacy in Primary Education and Martin Jenkins
for their invaluable input and guidance during the making of this book.

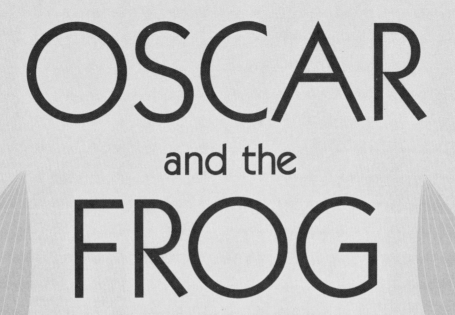

OSCAR
and the
FROG

A BOOK ABOUT GROWING

Geoff Waring

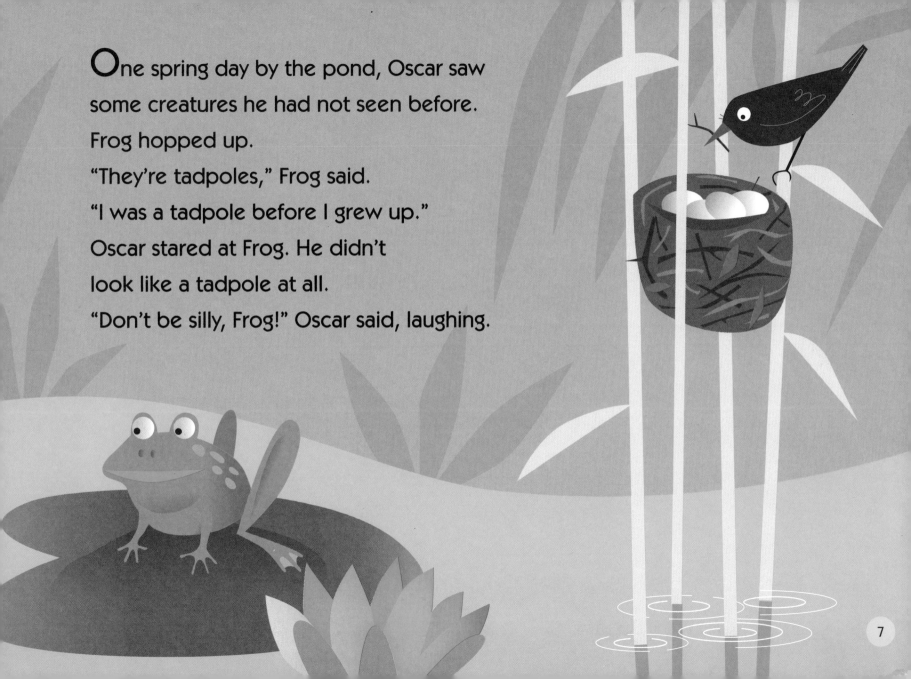

One spring day by the pond, Oscar saw
some creatures he had not seen before.
Frog hopped up.

"They're tadpoles," Frog said.

"I was a tadpole before I grew up."

Oscar stared at Frog. He didn't
look like a tadpole at all.

"Don't be silly, Frog!" Oscar said, laughing.

"It's true," Frog said, and he told Oscar how frogs grow.

"At first I looked like a dot in an egg. The egg was as soft as jelly.

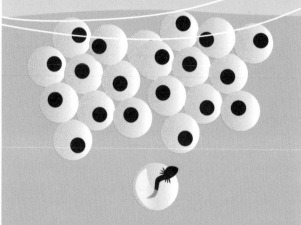

"I grew in the egg, then hatched out as a wriggly tadpole.

"I could breathe underwater through gills, like a fish.

"I was hungry for pondweed— it helped me to grow.

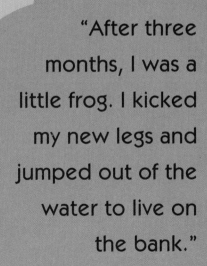

"Later my gills disappeared as I grew lungs to breathe air with. I grew back legs,

then front legs, and my tail started to shrink.

"After three months, I was a little frog. I kicked my new legs and jumped out of the water to live on the bank."

"What else hatches out of eggs?" Oscar asked. They looked in the pond. Frog showed Oscar some eggs that had been laid underwater.

Many water snails lay their eggs in pouches of jelly on stones or plants.

Dragonflies often lay their eggs on a plant stem just below the water.

Fish lay lots of eggs. The perch winds hers in long threads around plants, twigs, or stones.

They looked on the bank,
and Frog showed Oscar
some eggs that had been
laid where it's dry.

Many kinds of butterflies lay
their eggs on the undersides
of leaves. When the caterpillars
hatch out of the eggs, they
eat the leaves.

Many birds lay their eggs in nests high off the ground. Here the chicks will be safe from animals who might want to eat them when they hatch.

Ducks often nest on the ground close to water so their ducklings will be able to swim quickly away from danger.

13

"Do plants hatch out of eggs?" Oscar asked. "No," said Frog. "Most plants sprout from seeds. Each plant makes its own kind of seed."

The seeds of apple trees are stored inside their fruit.

Strawberry plants have small seeds on the outsides of their fruit.

Poppy plants have tiny seeds. They are light enough to be carried by the wind.

Coconuts are the seeds of coconut palm trees. They are huge and can float.

Most seeds ripen above the ground, but the seeds of the peanut plant grow in the earth.

"Did I hatch out of an egg, or did I sprout from a seed?" Oscar asked. "Neither," said Frog. "You were born. You looked a lot like you do now, only much smaller—with fur and paws, ears and a tail. You were hungry for milk from your mother!"

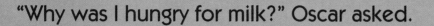

"Why was I hungry for milk?" Oscar asked.

"It helped you to grow," said Frog.

"Milk for you, pondweed for me . . .

leaves for these
caterpillars . . .

and bugs
for those
baby birds.
We all need
different
food to
grow."

19

Oscar stretched. "I am *so* big now," he told Frog. "But you're not as big as you will be," said Frog. "Are you?" asked Oscar. "Yes," Frog answered. "I've stopped growing now. I'm as big as I'm going to get."

21

"How long does it take to grow up?" Oscar asked.

"It depends," said Frog. "This flower will be full-grown in a few days . . .

but this young tree won't be tall until you are a very old cat."

"The baby birds will be as big as their parents next spring," Frog went on, "but the tadpoles will take three springs or more to be as big as I am. Each living thing takes its own time."

Just then, Oscar saw that his mother was coming.

"What about me?" he asked Frog.
"How long will I stay a kitten?"
"You will be a
full-grown cat
by winter," Frog
said, "as big as your
mother is now."

Oscar looked at
his mother. She
was much bigger
than he was.

"Don't be silly,
Frog!" he said, laughing.
"It's true," Frog said.
"Wait and see!"

Thinking about growing

By the pond, Oscar found out about these things:

Beginnings

Living things begin in
different ways.

Some hatch out
of eggs,

some sprout from
seeds,

and some are born.

How did you begin? On your next walk,
look for living things that
hatch, sprout, or are born.

Food

All living things have to eat to grow.
They need different kinds of food.

Pondweed

Leaves

Bugs

What helped you to grow when you
were very young? What do you eat
that helps you grow now?